PERFORMANCE MEASUREMENT
IN
LIBRARY AND INFORMATION SERVICES

GW00633156

Christine Abbott

The Aslib Know How Series
Editor : Sylvia P Webb

THE ASSOCIATION FOR INFORMATION MANAGEMENT

Published in 1994 by
Aslib, The Association for Information Management
Information House
20-24 Old Street
London EC1V 9AP

***

British Library Cataloguing in Publication Data
A catalogue record for this book is available from the British Library.
ISBN 0 85142 329 9

Aslib, The Association for Information Management, has some two thousand corporate members worldwide. It actively promotes better management of information resources.

Aslib lobbies on all aspects of the management of and legislation concerning information. It provides consultancy and information services, professional development training, specialist recruitment, and publishes primary and secondary journals, conference proceedings, directories and monographs.

Further information about Aslib can be obtained from :
Aslib, The Association for Information Management
Information House, 20-24 Old Street, London EC1V 9AP

Series Editor - Sylvia P. Webb

Sylvia Webb is a well known consultant, author and lecturer in the information management field. Her first book 'Creating an Information Service' was published by Aslib and has sold in over forty countries. She has experience of working in both the public and private sectors, ranging from public libraries to national and international organisations. She has also been a lecturer at Ashridge Management College, specialising in management and inter-personal skills, which led to her second book, 'Personal Development in Information Work', also published by Aslib. She has served on a number of government advisory bodies, is actively involved in professional education with Aslib and the Library Association and is also a former Vice-President of the Institute of Information Scientists.

*A list of titles in the Aslib Know How Series
appears on the back cover of this volume.*

Acknowledgements

My thanks are due to Sheila Corrall and Philip Payne for their helpful comments on parts of the text; also to Sheila Edginton, for her expert preparation of the diagrams.

Contents

1. Introduction

This guide is designed for those library professionals who appreciate the need to evaluate their services, but who are uncertain how to make the transition from theory to practice. In particular, it seeks to demonstrate how the development and use of performance indicators can and should be integrated into the management process. It provides a rationale, a framework within which performance indicators can be employed, and guidance on their implementation.

The subject of performance measurement in library and information services (LIS) is not new. Any library professional wishing to research the topic will quickly find a wealth of literature, dating from the late 1960s onwards. Approaches range from the highly theoretical to the detailed and practical. Some studies demand a sophisticated understanding of mathematical concepts; others pay little or no attention to statistical methods. What is clear however from all recent reviews of the literature (see, for example, Goodall (1) and Blagden (2)) is that work on the subject has been for the most part repetitive, with little attempt to build on previous work in the development of new approaches. Furthermore, published accounts have concentrated on what performance indicators are and what they can do; little attention has been given to assisting librarians with the (much more difficult) task of managing their implementation.

The widespread acceptance of the need for performance measurement and the plethora of writings on the topic contrast markedly with the small number of libraries in which performance measurement has been systematically implemented and maintained. There may be many reasons for this. Either librarians do not feel equipped with the requisite skills to undertake performance measurement, and hence feel unable to progress beyond the theory; or pressures of time, and the need to maintain the service on a day-to-day basis prevent them from undertaking such an initiative. Or perhaps they are intimidated by the effort required to develop performance indicators. So why, given this lack of progress at the practical level, does the theme of performance measurement continue to preoccupy librarians? Why do they persist in their concern with this topic?

As we shall see below, pressure to develop performance measurement has often come as much from forces outside the library or parent institution as from within it. Whatever the external pressures however, the most important and enduring argument in favour of performance measurement in any organisation is quite simply that it is an essential part of good management. Developing performance indicators should not be seen as a separate, self-contained activity, divorced from other aspects of management; performance indicators are integral to the management process, informing decisions, aiding the setting of objectives and priorities, providing explanations and evidence for courses of action, and helping to give direction and focus to the work of staff at all levels.

Although the terminology of performance measurement may often seem rarefied, the concept is quite straightforward. Performance indicators are, simply, management tools designed to assist library managers to determine how well the service is performing. They provide evidence on which to base judgements, but are not substitutes for that judgement, since performance data needs to be interpreted before such assessments can be made. In considering performance indicators, we are rarely dealing with absolutes. As Winkworth (3) helpfully reminds us, performance indicators are not an exact science. They help us to make relative and comparative judgements. However precise our calculations and however meticulous our data collection, the real skill of performance indicators is in their interpretation, and application. In Zweizig's (4) phrase, the role of performance indicators is "not to prove, but to improve".

2. Why measure performance?

In a seminal paper on evaluation and performance measurement in libraries published twenty years ago, Orr (5) distinguishes between evaluation based on how good a library is, and that based on how much good a library does. For many years the tendency in LIS publications such as annual reports (which has by no means disappeared) was for chief librarians to justify their libraries' 'goodness' in terms of a simple quantification of the activities they carried out. So, the inference went, a library which acquired five thousand books, or answered a thousand enquiries, or received ten thousand visitors must be a good one. And if the statistics had increased over the previous year, then that 'proved' that the library was getting even better than before.

What is missing from such a catalogue is any attempt to relate activity to needs, or services to demand; to assess the efficiency or effectiveness of the activities provided; or to question whether they are in fact the right activities, in the right balance. The hidden assumption in such statements is that libraries are a good thing; their existence does not need any further justification.

There are few librarians who would now assert that libraries need only justify their existence and argue their excellence in such terms. In the harsher economic climate which exists today, where competition for resources is fierce, there is an increasing acceptance that libraries must demonstrate their value in measurable ways. Performance measurement, as it is currently understood, attempts to help library managers, and their parent institutions, to assess libraries according to the good they do - the effectiveness, cost-effectiveness, and efficiency of their services.

The political imperative

As in many other areas of the public sector and service industries the initial driving force behind the introduction of performance indicators has been a political one. National political imperatives to encourage greater efficiency and accountability in public services have been a key factor here. As a consequence of such pressures there have been moves to impose the use of a prescribed set of performance indicators across whole sectors of library service. For example, in 1987 the CVCP (6) (Committee of Vice-Chancellors and Principals) recommended the use of a range of performance indicators which universities should collect and report centrally for annual publication. The indicators attracted much criticism, for three main reasons: firstly because of their partiality, being primarily input ratios (such as library expenditure per FTE (Full Time Equivalent) student; acquisitions expenditure per FTE student). So

3

while they reveal some information about how economical a given library is, they shed little light on its effectiveness or efficiency. Secondly the indicators are published annually as crude league tables, and have proved as controversial as league tables in other areas of public service. Finally the absence of any reference to local objectives in the publication of the league tables has meant that they are largely discredited with LIS professionals.

More recently, with the desire to see progress on this issue and in the interests of consistency, professional bodies such as COPOL, Council of Polytechnic Librarians, (Winkworth, (7)) and SCONUL, Standing Conference of National and University Libraries, (8) have worked to develop a coherent set of indicators for use in their respective sectors. 1993 saw the publication of a similar set of indicators for public libraries (Sumsion, (9)). While such initiatives can help to consolidate the best of current thinking and practice on the subject, their ultimate value is dependent on their degree of acceptability to practising librarians. (The particular difficulties of comparative indicators and league tables are discussed further in chapter 6).

Accountability to the parent institution

Libraries, in common with other service organisations, in both the public and the private sector, are increasingly required to justify the resources they consume, and demonstrate that the benefits derived are worth the expenditure. As well as describing the range, extent and importance of the services provided, libraries need to show that they are providing such services efficiently, and are not wasting resources - in other words, they must demonstrate that they offer not just value, but value for money.

As competition for resources becomes ever keener, libraries must convince their political masters of the importance of continuing to resource the library. This means demonstrating not so much the intrinsic quality of the library's services, (the library's 'goodness') but that the library is performing a useful, relevant and valuable function, without which the institution would be the poorer. Increasingly library managers are in the position of competing for resources with colleagues from other departments. Often their task is to persuade more senior colleagues that resources devoted to the library will bring more benefit to the institution than if those resources were to be given to another department. Performance indicators which illustrate the beneficial outcomes of providing given resources to the library can help in this essentially political negotiation process.

Performance indicators can also help library managers in situations in which they need to justify certain courses of action, or decisions. To document improvements in service using quantified performance data helps the prestige of the library, while any criticism which is made of the library is much more effectively deflected if hard data on performance is used, rather than vague generalisations.

Accountability to customers

A key aspect of good management is accountability to customers. The advent of customer or citizens' charters in the public sector, and the continuing importance of customer care considerations in all sectors, are encouraging libraries to publicise their standards of service - and such standards can best be established and monitored through the use of performance indicators. At the same time, users of service industries such as libraries are becoming increasingly discerning and critical. They are expecting these services, which traditionally are free at the point of use, to demonstrate the same efficiency and quality in their operations as commercial enterprises.

Performance indicators and service level agreements

Performance indicators are also important within the context of service level agreements (SLAs). In the public sector, in local authorities and in universities, the concept of SLAs is gaining currency. Briefly, an SLA can be described as an agreed, written contract which defines the services which a service department (such as library) will provide to a given client department, over a certain period, and, normally, for a certain price. The value of SLAs is that they enable clarification of the expectations, responsibilities and entitlements on both sides. In order for such agreements to be meaningful, standards of service must be written into the document. Here, as for customer charters, the only credible way to arrive at statements of standards is to develop performance indicators and monitor performance over a period of time.

Performance indicators and quality

Performance indicators also have value and relevance in the context of quality management and quality assurance. Quality assurance mechanisms attempt to define how a process will operate in order to ensure a given quality of product or service. Performance indicators attempt to measure to what extent that quality has been achieved. Neither quality assurance, nor performance indicators, guarantee quality. They are however complementary management tools.

5

Decision support

As has already been discussed, performance indicators are important to the library manager as aids to decision making, in areas such as resource allocation, priority setting, and planning future activity. For example, the use of performance indicators will help the library manager to:

- understand what the library is achieving

- monitor the library's progress year on year, and in comparison with other libraries or sites

- gauge how efficiently and effectively library operations and services are performing

- take decisions about future resourcing of service areas on the basis of hard information on past performance, rather than on intuition

- estimate the consequences of increasing or decreasing resources for the performance of different service areas

- check that the objectives of the library as a whole are accurately reflected in the balance of activity in the library.

Figure 1 illustrates the sorts of broad strategic questions which any senior manager is likely to ask in the course of managing the library. In deciding on appropriate courses of action, performance indicators can provide useful information on which to base one's judgements. How performance indicators fit into the planning cycle is discussed in chapter 4.

Performance measurement and performance appraisal

There is an important distinction to be made between performance measurement and performance appraisal. The premise of this guide is that performance measurement should be firmly service-focused, and not used to assess the performance of an individual member of library staff. This is an important point even in situations where one individual has sole responsibility for a specific service. Performance indicators are designed to enable library managers to make assessments about the success of their library services; they should not be thought of as means of staff assessment. Performance indicators can of course be used to assess comparative productivity, and there is certainly a relationship between staff appraisal and performance measurement. Any integrated planning and management process should ensure that individual work priorities are dictated by the same service priorities which underlie the development of performance indicators and that staff appraisal is directed towards helping the library as a whole to achieve its objectives. However, as management procedures, performance measurement and staff appraisal should be kept entirely separate.

How the library is performing

What the Chief Librarian needs to know

What is the optimal allocation of resources?
>between stock, staff, equipment
>between different services

How can the library achieve the optimal utilization of services/resources?
>optimal opening hours
>optimal layout of facilities

What is the best balance between the cost of service provision and the quality of service provision?
>speed
>amount
>standards

How well are we satisfying
>customers' needs?
>customers' demands?

Is this library more economical/efficient/effective
>than in previous years?
>than comparable libraries?

How well is the library fulfilling its mission / meeting its strategic objectives?

What level of market penetration is the library achieving?

Figure 1 - How the library is performing

3. Terminology

Statistics versus indicators

The terminology of performance assessment often deters library staff, and hampers their understanding of the essential concepts. The first distinction which needs to be made is between statistics and indicators. Simple quantification of activity - such as the number of book issues, the number of registered users of the library, the total annual visits to the library - are important figures for a manager to know, providing some insight into the size and scope of a given library's operation; but they do not facilitate any judgements as to the quality or performance of that library service. They are simply statistics. By contrast, a performance indicator is a quantitative expression of the use or value of an aspect of library service. Such indicators are usually derived by combining two statistics to form a ratio. So, the number of book loans can be divided by the number of registered library users to produce the ratio: average loans per registered borrower, which can be seen as an effectiveness indicator. Some studies, for example King Research Ltd (10), call statistics 'performance measures' and ratios 'indicators'. Other writers use only the word 'performance measures'. In this guide, the word 'statistic' is used for simple counts: 'measure' is avoided, as it suggests a degree of precision which is misleading. However, the term 'performance measurement' is used to describe the activity of using performance indicators, since no adequate alternative exists.

Libraries have always been good at quantifying their activities. The statistics which libraries publish most frequently are input statistics: the library budget, the number of staff employed, the number of journal subscriptions and the number of books purchased or the size of the acquisitions budget. But such statistics only tell the reader how well the library is resourced: they reveal nothing about the library's performance. Sometimes library annual reports contain information on library outputs: number of items catalogued, number of information skills seminars conducted and so forth. But here again the emphasis is on description, not analysis. In some cases comparative year-on-year data is provided which passes for performance information (for example 'library issues rose by five per cent on the previous year'). This figure in isolation does not demonstrate an improvement in performance. It could indeed illustrate increased effectiveness of services if the user population had remained static, or decreased. However, if the number of registered library borrowers had increased by ten per cent over the same period, or if the length of the loan period had been halved, then the statistics would take on a completely different meaning!

Evaluation and performance indicators

Confusion can also exist as to the difference between evaluation and performance indicators. Performance indicators clearly contribute to the process of evaluation, but the latter is a broader term for the assessment of performance. Some writers, such as Lancaster (11) approach evaluation of library services from the perspective of performance measurement, and use the sort of systematic approach to evaluation which is advocated here. But evaluation can also be purely subjective, and idiosyncratic. Evaluation, then, is the purpose of developing performance indicators: it does not of itself provide a methodology.

Standards, targets and performance indicators

The current interest in Citizens' Charters and quality assurance mechanisms has led to a renewed interest in the concept of standards. While there is clearly a link between performance indicators and standards, the link should be created at the stage of interpretation, not at the outset of the exercise. Indeed, to embark on the development of performance indicators with pre-conceived notions of standards or pre-established targets can be both misleading and counterproductive. More seriously, it can lead to disillusion and cynicism among staff. For example, a library manager who embarks on an analysis of the delivery times of inter-library loans, having previously made it clear that only a maximum delivery time of ten days is acceptable, is likely to be faced with one of three results: at one extreme, the staff concerned could refuse to cooperate; or they could cooperate cynically, and produce distorted and ultimately meaningless data, demonstrating that the standard is being achieved; or they could genuinely put all their energies into achieving the standard, to the detriment of other areas of service. Of course, if the standard set is lower than that which could be reached, then the exercise of gathering performance data will result in underachievement of the service's potential.

4. Prerequisites to performance measurement

One of the reasons why the copious literature on performance measurement may have failed to inspire LIS professionals is that the subject is often treated in isolation, unrelated to other aspects of the management process. Performance indicators have been seen as ends in themselves rather than as means to ends. This approach has had a number of consequences. It has led to a 'flavour of the month' approach to performance measurement, whereby institutions or their libraries have felt compelled to develop performance indicators without first considering the context in which they are being developed, and the real purpose of that development. The absence of context has made it difficult for library managers to act on the information emerging from the development of performance indicators. Moreover, when treated in isolation, there is little incentive for hard-pressed librarians to persevere with the collection and interpretation of performance data: they are unable to see how such effort can contribute to the improvement of the service they are managing.

To derive the maximum benefit from the development of performance indicators they should be firmly rooted within a strategic management and planning framework, as illustrated in Figure 2. In this model, performance indicators emerge from the definition of strategic objectives, and the results of performance measurement influence further strategic planning and strategic decisions.

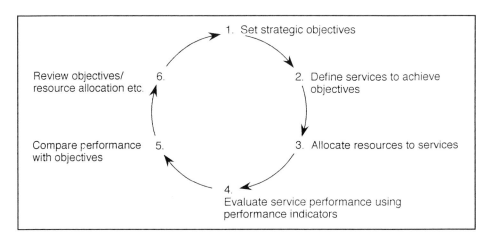

Figure 2 - Performance indicators in the planning cycle

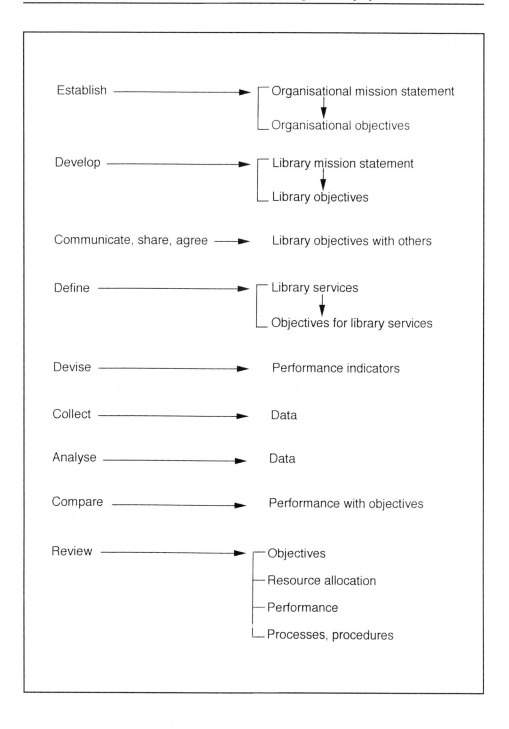

Figure 3 - Performance indicator route map

Meadows (12) endorses the advice of CIPFA, Chartered Institute of Public Finance and Accountancy, which suggests that the library manager should be able to answer the following questions before embarking on performance measurement:-

- what business are you in?
- what are you trying to achieve?

    what are your objectives?
    what targets have you set yourselves?

- within what constraints do you operate?
- how will you judge (or be judged) on your success, or otherwise?
- how is the libraries department (or library) structured?
- how is management control exercised?
- who are your customers/clients and what services do they require?

This list is helpful in focusing attention on ends, rather than means. However it still treats the library as a self-contained entity, divorced from the institutional context in which it operates. All libraries, even the largest national or research libraries, work within a framework established by a parent institution or governing body. As the model illustrated in Figure 3 suggests, it is the mission statement of the parent institution which should form the starting point for the development of library performance indicators.

Mission statements, while providing a useful initial focus, are often phrased in generalised and rather hyperbolic terms since their primary purpose is to define long-term aspirations. To be useful as management tools they must be followed by a statement of institutional objectives, which summarises what the institution is trying to achieve. So, for example, the mission statement for a university might be: 'To be a high-quality centre of teaching, research and learning.' This aspiration might translate into the following institutional objectives:-

- to provide a high-quality learning experience for undergraduate and postgraduate students in x subjects
- to be a centre of excellence in research in x subjects
- to contribute to the economic prosperity of the region by seeking opportunities for shared ventures with industry and commerce in the locality, to the mutual advantage of both parties.

For a private manufacturing company, the mission statement and corporate objectives are likely to be phrased in 'harder' language, and more quantifiable terms. The mission statement might encapsulate the company's desire to be a leader in its particular niche market, and the institutional objectives might refer primarily to concepts such as market share, customer/brand loyalty and, perhaps, to the company ethos for service, or quality.

Before embarking on the development of performance indicators, it is essential for the LIS manager to know and understand the mission and objectives of the parent institution. In cases where the parent body has not developed explicit formulations for either its mission or its objectives, it is still important for the library manager to be as clear as possible as to what the objectives and mission are, for they will nevertheless exist in the minds of the chief executives of that institution and will, consciously or unconsciously, influence the assessment they make of the library's performance. This may involve developing your own formulation, and consulting a number of senior managers in the institution for their reactions. (For more guidance on strategic planning and the development of mission statements and objectives, see Strategic planning for library and information services, by Sheila Corrall, also in this series).

The library mission statement

The same requirement to determine what one is trying to achieve pertains at the level of the library. The library must itself develop a mission statement, and a series of strategic objectives. In order for the library to be able to demonstrate its accountability, the library's objectives should relate back to the overall objectives of the institution.

As Figure 3 indicates, the objectives also serve as a basis for defining the services to be provided by the library. Having agreed the library's objectives, it is then often helpful to review the services the library provides, to ensure that all major services can be related back to the objectives. For, if a given service cannot be shown to support any of the overarching objectives of the library, it is fair to ask why the library is investing resources in that service.

Thus the statement of library objectives provides the framework within which performance indicators should be developed. And as Figure 2 illustrates, the planning process involving objective setting, resource allocation and performance evaluation is not linear, but cyclical. Performance indicators are both informed by and inform the strategic objectives.

13

5. The library as a system

In considering how to approach performance measurement, it is important to ensure that any assessment encompasses all the roles which the library performs. To do this it is helpful to think of the library in system terms. This analysis is based on Brophy (13).

The library as a physical system

Most library and information serices exist as physical systems, that is, they consist of physical spaces, which can be visited, used for reference, study, to find information, and so on. While there has been undue concentration over the years on this aspect of the library at the expense of others, it is nevertheless important to consider the use of the library building or area in any system of performance measurement.

The library as a collection

A second conceptual model of a library is as a collection of materials. Again, most librarians would consider this definition too limiting as a total expression of what a library does, but it is also true that for many library users, particularly perhaps those in academic institutions, the size, scope and currency of the collections of material are more important than any other aspect of service. Increasingly of course the term 'library materials' must be extended to incorporate information services which are available in electronic form, whether on CD-ROM or on-line.

The library as an information gateway

One can also consider a library as an information gateway - a means by which users are put in touch with the information they require but which is held elsewhere. This does not just mean the use of information technology to access remote databases, but also the use of inter-library loan, referral services, and the assistance provided by reference librarians in enabling users to find their way through complex reference sources. Within this conceptual model the role of library staff is to retrieve the necessary information, direct users to it, and to use their professional expertise to help them navigate effectively through the information maze.

Other roles which a library performs may depend upon the particular sector in which it operates. So, a commercial company library might have a key role as a collator and disseminator of information, placing emphasis on customised, targeted services such as current awareness bulletins and SDI, designed to save the library user time. An academic library might see itself as (to use Brophy's term) an 'agent of learning'. This would include the provision of an environment which facilitates self-directed learning, teaching the skills of information retrieval and information management. A public library may wish to define a role for itself as a leisure facility, a means of enabling and encouraging recreational pursuits, such as the loan of audio cassettes, compact discs, and paintings, or the holding of art exhibitions and concerts.

The reason for considering the various roles of your library before embarking on the development of performance indicators is that to do so provides a checklist, a way of ensuring that any set of performance indicators reflects the totality of your library's activity, not only parts of it. It can be particularly valuable to undertake an exercise of this sort with a group or groups of staff. If staff have never undertaken such an exercise, it will help to stimulate their thinking as to the real purpose of the library. This will pave the way for further work on strategic planning, and for the development of performance indicators for the different service areas.

15

6. Types of indicator

In manuals of performance measurement it is common to see conceptual models of libraries as a series of processes, similar to that in Figure 4. Such models provide a useful way of visualising what the library does, and also form a framework around which performance indicators can be constructed.

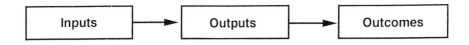

Figure 4 - Conceptual model of a library - 1

The different elements in the model can be defined as follows:-

Inputs: those resources, such as staff, materials, and capital funding, which are put into a library's operation.

Outputs: the direct products of a library's operation, or the activities it carries out. Outputs can be quantified, in terms such as number of loan transactions, enquiries answered, materials catalogued, exhibitions held, seminars conducted and so on.

Outcomes: these are the uses made by the consumer of a given output, and the degree of satisfaction felt with those outputs.

Inputs, outputs and outcomes are to a greater or lesser extent within the control of the library, or at least of its funding body. Beyond the control of the library itself lie other data elements, knowledge of which is important to the library manager in the context of performance measurement. These include basic statistics about the user population, locality and environment. Such data are 'givens', representing constraints on the library's operation, and hence are essential pieces of information in the performance indicator jigsaw. Here they are called 'environmental statistics'. Examples include:

- total population size
- total number of registered users
- geographical distribution of population
- geographical distribution of users
- population characteristics
- user characteristics.

Population means the total number of potential users of the library, such as the regional population (in the case of a public library), the number of staff and students (for an educational library) or the total number of employees (in the case of a company library). It is also important to know the total number of library users. (There is of course a difference between registered users and active users. The former statistic is normally available from the library's own data files, but it may only be possible to find out the latter through surveys and questionnaires.)

Geographical distribution of population is of most importance in public library systems with a network of branch libraries, but it could also be relevant to educational institutions on split sites, or libraries in large companies which are either multi-site, or cover a considerable geographical catchment area.

Population characteristics will include age, sex, social class, occupation (for public libraries); status (ie student or member of academic staff) subject or department, year of study (for educational libraries); and job type, site or area of work, in the case of company libraries.

Beyond outcomes one can note less tangible areas of performance, sometimes referred to as higher order effects (10). These have to do with the ultimate purpose of the library, the extent to which the service affects the community being served. Those who wish to evaluate the higher order effects of libraries usually do so via so-called impact indicators. So, for example, if a university library wished to assess the impact of introducing a particular service it might wish to study the correlation between use of that service and the instances of degrees passed with first class honours. Similarly public libraries wishing to assess their impact could look for example at the relationship between use of the library's collections of careers materials by the unemployed, and the instances of those users finding jobs.

It is generally accepted however that attempts to assess the higher order effects of libraries by means of performance indicators are fraught with difficulty. A range of variables affect the relationship between the library services and its higher order effects, most of which are outside the library's control. For example, there are clearly a number of factors which determine whether a student will gain a first class honours degree or not, or whether an unemployed person finds a job, which have nothing to do with their use of library services. Consequently, impact indicators are difficult to interpret and act upon and are best dealt with as part of statements of strategic aims and mission. For the purposes of this guide, they will be largely ignored.

The different elements in the conceptual model - environmental statistics, inputs, outputs and outcomes - operate in certain relationships to each other and can be compared in different ways. It is the relationships between the different elements which form the focus for performance measurement, as Figure 5 illustrates. The relationships are here defined as: economy, market penetration, efficiency, effectiveness, cost-effectiveness, costs and productivity.

Performance indicators are created by comparing the data elements in different combinations. The indicators can be variously described. This guide identifies fourteen essential indicators, at three broad levels. While they may not be the only indicators a library manager will wish to use, they are considered the most important; other indicators will tend to be refinements of these basic fourteen. They are discussed in more detail later in this chapter. The three levels, the generic indicators, and the attributes they indicate are illustrated in Figure 6.

The relationship between outputs and inputs provides two types of indicator. Firstly one can assess how efficiently an operation is carried out, from the customer's point of view. So *efficiency indicators* will most often be expressed in terms of the speed of supply of a service. Examples of efficiency indicators are:-

- throughput times for processes such as acquisitions and cataloguing etc.

- delivery times, for inter-library loans, acquisitions, answering of telephone reference enquiries and so on.

Secondly, the relationship between outputs and inputs can be used to generate information on the productivity of different services, and on costs. Such indicators can be grouped together as *operational performance indicators*. They tend to apply at the sub-service level of discrete activities. Examples include:

- average number of transactions (such as loans transactions, enquiries answered, or on-line searches conducted) per relevant member of LIS staff

- unit costs of transactions or activities, such as the cost per enquiry answered, or the cost per new catalogue record created.

18

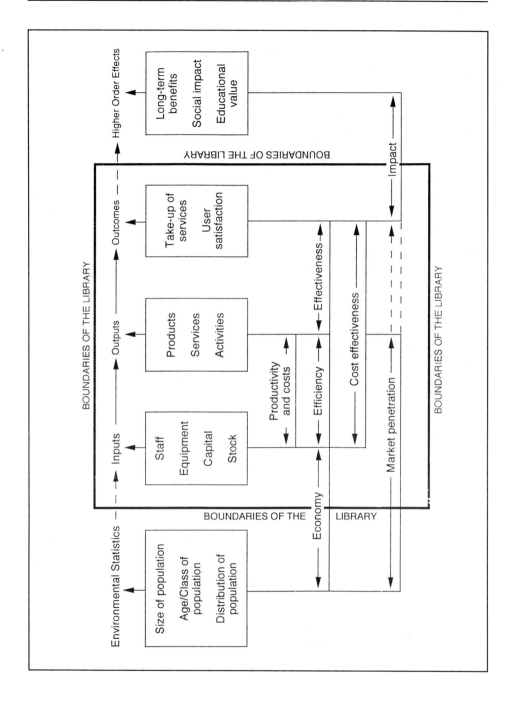

Figure 5 - Conceptual model of a library - 2

Level	Attribute	Generic performance indicators
Macro	Economy	1. Resources committed per 100 population / 100 users
		2. Proportion of budget committed
	Market penetration	3. Registered users (of the library / specific service) as a proportion of population
		4. Correlation between registered users' profiles and population profile
		5. Take-up of specific services
Service	Efficiency	6. Speed of supply, delivery, throughput
	Effectiveness	7. Turnover rate
		8. Timeliness of supply / product delivery
		9. Accuracy of supply / product delivery
		10. Failure rate/needs fill rate
	Cost-effectiveness	11. Cost per use / output / user of a given level of service
		12. Cost of service compared with degree of market penetration
Operational	Costs	13. Unit cost per output
	Productivity	14. Outputs per relevant staff member

Figure 6 - Levels of indicator

Looking at the relationship between library inputs and environmental statistics indicators of how economical a library operation is may be generated, eg:-

- library expenditure per head of population/student/ member of staff (of a company)

- acquisitions expenditure per user

- library staff per 100 library population.

A further indicator of economy is:

- proportion of budget consumed by a given service.

Indicators of economy are normally considered in relation to the library as a whole, but may also be valuable at the service level, for example when the introduction of a new service is being considered, or the re-evaluation of an existing one is taking place; or when a library manager is conducting an options analysis of various methods of information provision. For instance, a library manager who is considering alternative models for providing access to an on-line information service may wish to consider among other things the proportion of the relevant budget which would be consumed by the different options. For a method of access which is highly efficient and effective but absorbs 99 per cent of the total on-line budget is unlikely to be a realistic option.

While in isolation indicators of economy give no insight into how well the library is performing, it is useful to monitor them over time, and to compare the same indicators at different sites within the same library system. They can often be of most value as possible explanations for other indicators: for example, from other studies you may discover that customers are waiting increasingly long times in queues at various service desks, and that the number of customers has increased over time. In today's climate, it is highly unlikely that the increased demand has been matched automatically by increased staff resources for the library, leading to the reduced efficiency observed. If the librarian is able to demonstrate this to the advisory committee or funding body it may at the very least help to forestall criticism of the service; if one is extremely fortunate it might lead to an increase in the number of library staff.

A comparison of outputs or outcomes with environmental statistics provides indicators of *market penetration*. As with indicators of economy, such indicators normally operate at the macro-level of the whole library service, for example:-

- number of registered users as a percentage of total potential users

- degree of correlation between population characteristics and user characteristics: (if some key groups are seriously under-represented, it is worth investigating possible reasons for this).

However market penetration indicators can also relate to the take-up of specific services, for example:

- percentage of first year student population who attend induction tours
- percentage of potential market who make use of a current awareness service.

Effectiveness indicators are generated by relating outcomes to outputs, from the perspective of the user of those outputs. Some effectiveness indicators consist of indirect measures, such as the turnover rate of stock and the accuracy or timeliness of supply of a product or service. The logic of such indicators is that the more heavily stock is used (ie how many times it is 'turned over' in a year), or the greater the accuracy which is achieved in the supply of a product or service, the more effective that service must be in meeting the needs or demands of the library's customers.

However for any library manager the best measure of the effectiveness of a service must be the actual satisfaction which users feel with that service. So the majority of effectiveness indicators require the librarian to obtain direct feedback from users. The most commonly used indicators of user satisfaction involve either measures of failure rate, or its inverse, needs fill rate. Failure rate measures assess the extent to which customers fail to find what they want, and tend to be quantitative in nature; needs fill rate studies focus on the extent to which customers' expressed needs (or demands) are met by library services. Needs fill rate studies tend to provide more qualitative information. Comparing the number of stock items users find on the shelf (or in the library catalogue) with the number they were seeking on entering or contacting the library is a well-known measure of failure rate. More qualitative and subjective feedback can be obtained by asking users themselves to rate their degree of satisfaction with a service. User satisfaction questionnaires and similar tools provide the most appropriate means of obtaining this type of information. Questionnaires are explored further in chapter 8.

Cost-effectiveness indicators are also derived by relating inputs to outcomes, but in a slightly more sophisticated way. They compare the effectiveness achieved in providing a given level of service with the cost of achieving that service level; or the cost of providing a service with the number of active users (the degree of market penetration) of that service. They can assist in situations where a library manager needs to decide if the benefit derived from a service justifies the level of resource allocated to it; or to assess the increased benefit which could be derived by enhancing an existing service.

Such categorisations of performance indicators can prove helpful to library managers, by ensuring that the indicators selected for investigation actually relate to the characteristic being measured. However to see such groupings as immutable is to become diverted by the theory: they are largely conveniences. In particular, the dividing line between efficiency and effectiveness is often blurred, since the efficiency of a service is likely to contribute as much towards a user's satisfaction with it as its effectiveness. For example, a manager wishing to investigate the degree of user satisfaction with a photocopying service, an issue desk or enquiry service, might conduct observations to establish the average amount of time customers spend queuing for the service. Strictly speaking, these observations provide information on service efficiency, since they concern the speed of delivery of a service. Yet common sense suggests that from such an indicator some assessment of user satisfaction could be made: as a rule, the more efficiently one is served, the more satisfied one is. In many instances it is the use of a range of indicators which proves valuable to the manager, since together the indicators help the manager to build up a picture of that service, of its merits, shortcomings and areas where improvement is needed. As we discuss in chapter 8, carrying out user questionnaires is time-consuming, so the judicious use of such indirect indicators of effectiveness can save valuable time.

As Figure 6 shows, indicators can be grouped at three levels. These levels represent a hierarchy, as depicted in Figure 7.

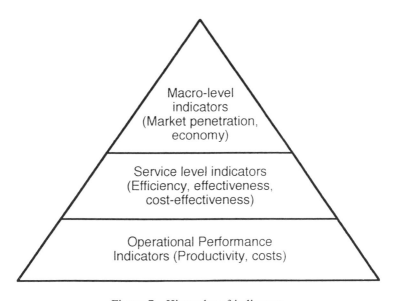

Figure 7 - Hierarchy of indicators

At the top of the pyramid are the macro-level indicators, which relate to the library as a whole. As has already been mentioned these will tend to be predominantly indicators of economy, having to do with how much resource is put into a library, but will also include indicators of market penetration. In the second tier are service level indicators, which focus on specific services

23

within the library, normally in terms of efficiency, effectiveness and cost-effectiveness. At the bottom level are operational performance indicators, which seek to provide information on productivity and costs. As with the types of indicator such groupings are largely a convenience, and some shading exists between one group and another.

In any assessment of performance, one indicator alone is rarely sufficient; a range of indicators must be considered in combination, as is illustrated in the following example; a library manager wishing to evaluate the performance of a recently-introduced self-service CD-ROM information service may use the following indicators :

- proportion of CD-ROM budget committed (Economy)

- actual users as a proportion of potential users (Market penetration)

- time spent per user per session (Efficiency)

- unit cost per user session (Costs)

- proportion of first time users who are repeat users (Indirect measure of user satisfaction - ie Effectiveness)

- subjective user satisfaction ratings (Direct measure of user satisfaction - ie Effectiveness)

- cost per user of meeting information needs in this way (Cost effectiveness)

Different types of indicator adopt a different perspective when answering the question: how well does the library perform? It follows that different types of indicators will prove more significant to the library manager at different times, depending on the purpose and the need. For example, a university library faced with large increases in student numbers will find it useful to have information on the number of customers served at the issue desk per member of staff, at various times of day (an operational performance indicator of productivity) in order to provide evidence of the additional staff resource which may be required to deal with such an increase. However the library manager who is examining user satisfaction and ways of improving customer care may wish primarily to see indicators of the efficiency and effectiveness of the issue desk services: studies of average queue lengths and waiting periods and direct user feedback will prove useful in this context.

24

For the library paymaster ...

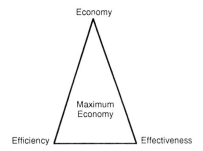

For the library user ...

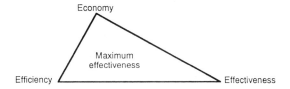

For the library manager ...

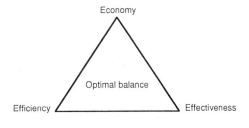

Figure 8 - Satisfaction with the library

As Figure 8 illustrates, different stakeholder groups will tend to place emphasis on different service attributes, depending on their perspective. Library paymasters are, arguably, most interested in indicators of economy - in other words how cheaply the library service can be provided. Library users will be keenest on efficiency and effectiveness indicators; for a library user the ideal library is one in which all items required are available 100 per cent of the time; in which queues at the library service desk do not exist and waiting times for inter-library loans are minimal. Such a library service could however be totally uneconomic. The role of the library manager, therefore, is to balance the users' needs for an effective service and the requirement of the funding body for an economical one with a third requirement - that of efficiency of operations - and so provide a library service which, from all perspectives, represents value for money. A well managed library will be one in which the optimum balance between these three requirements is achieved and demonstrated. Performance indicators will not tell the library manager what the optimum balance is. They will however provide the information from which judgements can be made as to the best balance for the local situation, and evidence to use in defending those judgements.

Criteria for performance indicators

For performance indicators to have credibility as aids to decision making, they must conform to certain criteria. The following list is adapted from Ford (14).

- relevance (or appropriateness): the indicator must be relevant to the area of service being analysed

- helpfulness: the indicator must be informative, and must enable potential problem areas to be highlighted

- validity: the indicator must measure what it is supposed to measure, and not something else

- reliability: the indicator must remain reliable over time, and not contain flaws which will invalidate it

- practicality: the indicator must be practical in terms of the cost of collection, both for library staff and for users.

These criteria may seem obvious. However, a number of indicators recommended for use in certain manuals contravene at least one of these criteria. For example, one of the performance indicators recorded by Sumsion (9) for measuring value for money in public libraries is 'lending costs per issue' (an indicator of economy). In Scotland, despite professional objections, this is measured as 'total staff costs per item issued'. The danger of such a method of measurement is that a library operation which undertakes a wide variety of activities other than lending would be unfairly penalised, since the staff overhead costs of providing a range of services would be attributed to just one aspect of service - lending. This indicator would appear to contravene the validity criterion.

26

Comparative indicators

The problems caused by publishing league tables of performance indicator information, particularly sets of indicators which have been imposed from outside, have been mentioned in chapter 2. For the library manager a threat which can result from such league tables is the appearance of what Brophy (13) has called 'the creeping mean'. This means that any library which reveals expenditure above the mean average in the league table is likely to come under pressure from the senior management in that institution to explain the reasons for its apparent profligacy, and probably to reduce expenditure to bring it closer to the mean. As a consequence, the mean average in the league tables moves inexorably downwards, as those above the average are forced closer to the mean.

There are nevertheless some situations in which comparative indicators are valuable. This is particularly so in large library systems which operate on a number of different sites. In these cases it can be legitimate and instructive to compare similar statistics and performance indicators in different locations. There are however three important points to remember when using performance indicators comparatively:-

- Compare like with like, for example:

    if measuring book issues per registered borrower, are loan periods the same length in both sites?

    are renewals treated in the same way?

- Take local circumstances into account when interpreting the comparative data, for example:

    if comparing the proportion of staff who make use of a company library in two sites, do both sites contain similar proportions of different types and grades of staff?

    do both sites provide equal opportunities for access to the library, either in person or by remote electronic access?

    are there differences in shift patterns, or in the type of location (eg between a city centre and a 'green-field' site) which could impact on the use of the library?

- Do not publish the comparative data until points 1 and 2 above have been dealt with adequately

This last point is most important. If staff believe that performance data will be published as crude league tables, either without any explanation or without an opportunity for internal consideration beforehand, then they will become disillusioned with the project. Those responsible for collecting the data required may be tempted to falsify or 'touch up' the data to cast themselves in a more favourable light. And without genuine data, any performance measurement exercise is valueless.

Service level and operational performance indicators

The majority of indicators become most meaningful when applied to specific services. The exact areas of service which a library will choose to evaluate will depend on the type of library or information service, the services provided, the way services are organised, and the context in which the library operates. However, there are a number of generic library services which are common to the vast majority of libraries. On the following pages each of these generic services is analysed in terms of its broad scope and definition, the types of indicators needed and any particular points to note relating to performance measurement. Very specialised services which exist only in one sector (for example mobile library services, which are the unique province of the public library service) have been omitted from this list.

While the exact scope and definition of these services might not be applicable in every library, this list provides a framework which individual library managers can adapt to suit their own situation. As well as service level indicators, operational performance indicators are covered, since productivity and costs are aspects of service which the library manager will wish to measure in relation to specific service areas, or indeed to the discrete activities which go to make up those services.

Increasingly the services listed are computer-based, or have computerised elements to them. Monitoring the performance of those computer systems is an important aspect of the manager's job. In some organisations guidelines covering procurement and capital expenditure require purchasers of expensive pieces of equipment to report formally on the performance of such equipment. Since performance appraisal of equipment is outside the scope of this guide, references to it have been omitted from the analysis of service areas below, but library managers will wish to include performance evaluation of the relevant computer hardware and software as part of service evaluation. For example, for any issue service, inter-library loans service, or cataloguing facility which is computer-based, the library manager will wish to be kept informed on the systems down-time and the consequent non-availability and reduced efficiency/effectiveness of the service. Performance of other types of equipment, such as photocopy machines and audio-visual equipment, needs to be monitored in a similar way.

28

Acquisitions

Definition and scope
The process by which library materials (books, journals, electronic information services, audio-visual materials, pamphlets, reports, standing orders etc.) are ordered and acquired for the library stock.

Performance indicators

Efficiency:	speed of supply
Effectiveness:	accuracy of supply
Costs:	unit cost of supply
Productivity:	items processed per relevant member of staff

Analysis of the acquisitions function will need to be subdivided according to material type - journals, monographs, CD-ROM services etc., and in cases where procedures for acquiring national and foreign materials differ.

Analysis of the timeliness of supply (an effectiveness indicator) may need to include both the time taken at the acquisitions stage and at the cataloguing stage, since from the users' point of view both represent behind the scenes processes which must normally be completed before they can receive the item requested.

Cataloguing and classification

Definition and scope
The provision of accurate, appropriate descriptive records of all the library's holdings of materials, enabling users to locate materials in the library catalogue, by author, title, and subject; and to find those materials on the library shelves.

Performance indicators

Efficiency:	delay time/throughput
Effectiveness:	accuracy of service
	timeliness of supply
	user failure rate at the catalogue/shelf
Cost-effectiveness:	cost of different levels of cataloguing (compared with user failure rates at the catalogue/shelf)
Costs:	unit cost of cataloguing and classification
Productivity:	items catalogued/classified per relevant member of staff

Analysis of the cataloguing and classification   functions will need to be subdivided according to material type - journals, monographs, pamphlets etc., and by other operating variables eg the language in which the item is written.

29

Analysis of the timeliness of supply (an effectiveness indicator) may need to include both the time taken at the acquisitions stage and at the cataloguing stage, since from the users' point of view both represent behind the scenes processes which must normally be completed before they can receive the item requested.

For a more detailed discussion of how to analyse the performance of a cataloguing department, see Abbott (15).

Processing

Definition and scope
The means by which materials acquired by the library are prepared for the shelves, including binding, labelling and shelf marking.

Performance indicators

Efficiency:	delay time/throughput
Effectiveness:	accuracy of service
Costs:	unit cost of processing an item
Productivity:	items processed per relevant member of staff

If external binding companies are used, then records of the costs of binding and the time each consignment takes to complete will be needed as supporting data.

Collection maintenance

Definition and scope
Reshelving or refiling of material returned from loan/used within the library/ new material. Shelf checking and tidying; shelf guiding; stock moves.

Performance indicators

Efficiency:	proportion of service hours material is off the shelves/unavailable
Effectiveness:	accuracy of shelving, guiding
	ease of use (of collections)
Costs:	unit cost of shelving an item
Productivity:	items shelved per relevant member of staff

Since the ease of use indicator seeks to assess how successful users are at finding the material they want, it is an inverse measure of user failure rates. Feedback from users will be required in order to gain this information. A study of user failure rates can be undertaken to provide a range of performance information, on shelving, guiding and collection development. Spot checks can be used to assess the accuracy of shelving and shelf tidying.

30

Collection development (including selection, deselection, and relegation)

Definition and scope
The provision of materials to meet customers' needs/demands in the right quantities at the right time.

Performance indicators

Economy:	proportion of library budget committed
Effectiveness:	turnover rate: average number of issues/uses per item (by subject)
	proportion of purchase requests satisfied (by subject)
	items on loan as a proportion of total stock (by subject)
Cost-effectiveness:	cost of stock/collections per user
Costs:	unit cost of selecting, deselecting and relegating an item
	average cost per item purchased (by subject), compared with external indices

Analysis of collection development will need to be subdivided according to material type - journals, monographs, CD-ROM services etc., and by subject category.

Analysis of in-house use of materials in an open-access collection poses a particular problem. One possible means of gathering such data is to take an area of stock, ask users not to refile items they have used from that area for a given period, and to count the number of items removed from the shelves each day. Alternatively, the widely accepted rule of thumb that the ratio of in-house uses to issues is approximately 3:1 could be used. Neither method is entirely satisfactory, but both are probably good enough approximations.

Gathering performance data on the use of electronic information services is often easier than for stock in hard copy. Firstly, the systems themselves, whether on-line or CD-ROM, often retain data on number of uses, usage time, and costs of use. Given the high costs of such services, cost-effectiveness measures may be very important here, and asking users for feedback is the only satisfactory way to gather the necessary data.

Information skills training

Definition and scope
The provision of individual/small group training on techniques of library use, information retrieval, and information management in support of their study/teaching/learning/research/business/leisure needs.

Performance indicators

Market penetration: actual users as proportion of potential users
Effectiveness: needs fill rate /user satisfaction with training
percentage repeat use
Cost-effectiveness: cost per user (compared with extent of market penetration/staff time spent on this service)
Costs: unit cost per training session provided
Productivity: number of training sessions run per relevant member of staff

The concept of information skills training is most widely understood in academic libraries. It includes induction tours, one-to-one training on specific information sources, group tuition on information retrieval and information management techniques and instruction on the use of information retrieval tools and packages. Increasingly however similar training is being undertaken in special libraries. The range of activities covered within information skills training would normally need to be evaluated separately.

In academic libraries and some special libraries such as legal practices information skills training is sometimes allied to study skills training, which is not covered here.

Mediated on-line searching

Definition and scope
Search and retrieval of references/information from remote on-line databases in support of specific information needs.

Performance indicators

Economy: proportion of budget committed
Market penetration: actual users as proportion of potential users
Efficiency: time taken per search
Effectiveness: surveys of needs fill rate
percentage of repeat use
Cost-effectiveness: cost per user (compared with extent of market penetration/staff time spent on this service)
relationship between time taken and references retrieved from different databases
Costs: unit cost per search
Productivity: number of searches conducted per relevant member of staff

In commercial libraries the most important indicator of the performance of the on-line searching service may be a value-added measure: such as the extent to which undertaking the search saves the end-user time, saves duplication and loss of productivity for the organisation, or reduces the uncertainty factor in a given strategic or commercial decision. Such analyses are difficult to calculate in a meaningful way (being, like all impact measures, somewhat hypothetical in nature). Also, it is easier to consider value-added measures in relation to the library as a whole, at the macro-level, than in relation to specific services, although an attempt could be made to obtain such evaluation through user questionnaires or surveys.

Traditionally, the ratio of relevance to retrieval has been used as an indicator of the performance of on-line searches, and on-line databases. This is however a problematic method, since it implies the existence of an optimum ratio between the two, and furthermore assumes that the client knows what this optimum is. It also ignores the fact that, in some situations, particularly in a commercial environment, or in certain specialised areas such as patents searching, the value of retrieving zero information about a product or initiative can be of considerably greater value than retrieving a large number of references, however relevant. For this reason, it is suggested here that the best way to obtain data on effectiveness is to ask the clients for feedback.

Note that end-user searching of self-service electronic databases is included under collection development. Depending on local circumstances, libraries may wish to group services in another way.

Publications

Definition and scope
Provision of leaflets, guides, and handouts enabling customers to make best use of the library's services, or informing them of specific activities and services available.

Performance indicators

Economy:	proportion of budget committed
Market penetration:	proportion/range of customers using the publications
Efficiency:	average preparation/production time
Effectiveness:	turnover rate of stocks
Cost-effectiveness:	cost per publication of different standards of production
Costs:	unit cost per leaflet

Turnover rate is an effectiveness indicator of the demand for and take-up of publications. It is of course important to eliminate any extraneous variables from the analysis: for example, in one academic library, it was discovered that the extremely high take-up of leaflets was due at least in part to the fact that they were single sided, and hence students used the backs for their own personal printing! Once this variable had been eradicated (by overprinting the backs) genuine data on take-up could be obtained.

An additional way of measuring the effectiveness of publications is to ask users for feedback. This might best be done as part of a larger user satisfaction questionnaire, covering a range of inter-related information services.

Usage of space

Definition and scope
Provision within the library building or designated library space of facilities for study, browsing, relaxation and use of services and equipment.

Performance indicators

> Market penetration: annual number of visits per head of population
> Effectiveness: seat occupancy: Proportion of seats/study places etc. occupied
> Cost-effectiveness: cost per user of different models of opening hours
> Costs: cost per user/per visit/ per opening hour of maintaining the library building/area
> cost per square metre of library space

The importance attached to this indicator will depend upon the nature of the library and its environment, and on the outcome of the analysis of the library as a system (chapter 5). It is an important indicator for any large public or academic institution, in which library use normally requires a personal visit, and in which significant resources are committed to maintaining the building and its facilities. It may be less significant for a company or special library, where the library often exists primarily as an information gateway rather than a physical entity, and where the primary means of access may be by telephone or by other means eg electronic mail. However for commercial organisations in which the library occupies a significant amount of space cost per square metre is likely to be the most relevant costs measure.

Cost-effectiveness indicators in this area have most relevance when changing profiles of library opening are under consideration. For example, a user survey may show that a certain proportion of those surveyed want extended opening at the weekends, while others want extended opening on weekday evenings. A cost-benefit analysis of the various models available can shed light on the best option to select by demonstrating the relationship between the proportion of users who might be satisfied by a given model of extended opening, and the costs of so doing.

Inter-library loans (borrowing)

Definition and scope
Provision of a document supply system for obtaining items which are not held in the library, either for loan or photocopy.

Performance indicators

    Economy: proportion of budget committed
    Market penetration: take-up of the service
    Efficiency: speed of supply
    Effectiveness: timeliness of supply
                         accuracy of supply
    Costs: unit cost per item requested
                         unit cost per item received
    Productivity: items processed per relevant member of staff

Speed of supply and timeliness of supply are related indicators, and similar data are needed for both. However the former is an efficiency indicator, which measures how quickly an item is delivered; the latter indicates service effectiveness, since it is a subjective measure of the extent to which the item is delivered at the right time for the user.

In interpreting the analysis of inter-library loans it would be important to distinguish between different request types (journal article, conference report, monograph) as well as the source of supply. Libraries which undertake significant inter-library lending may wish to include analyses of its performance under this heading.

Issue services

Definition and scope
Provision of a system enabling registered or bona fide library users to borrow items from stock to use outside the library building/area.

Performance indicators

    Market penetration: take-up of the service: average loans/transactions per
                              registered user per month/year
    Efficiency: transactions per service hour
                         average waiting time
    Effectiveness: accuracy of the service (eg incidence of mistakes)
    Costs: cost per transaction
                         cost per service hour
    Productivity: transactions per relevant member of staff

In many libraries, apart from large public and academic lending libraries, issue desk services are combined with other services - such as borrower registration, fax services, and enquiry services. Library managers may wish to group all these front-line services together for evaluation purposes, or distinguish between them.

In some libraries issue desk services are part of a broader function of document delivery (ie delivery of items from remote store or closed stack). Such services could be evaluated along with the issue desk services, or treated separately.

Enquiry work

Definition and scope
The provision to customers of essential support in using library collections by answering/providing guidance on quick reference enquiries, assisting with catalogue searches and location of materials, providing advice on information sources and search strategies; answering reference enquiries, and providing referrals to specialist sources.

Performance indicators

Economy:	proportion of budget committed
Market penetration:	actual users as proportion of potential users
Efficiency:	enquiries answered per service hour
	average waiting time
Effectiveness:	surveys of needs fill rate (user satisfaction)
Cost-effectiveness:	cost per user/per service hour of different profiles of service provision
Costs:	cost per enquiry answered
	cost per service hour
Productivity:	enquiries answered per relevant member of staff

One way of assessing the effectiveness of reference services is to use obtrusive or unobtrusive testing. Neither method is advocated here; testing implies a view of reference and enquiry services which is increasingly simplistic, for it assumes that in reference work there is an objectively right and a wrong answer to the questions being asked. While in some reference services a proportion of enquiries may conform to this view (eg "What is the capital of Zimbabwe?"), the majority of reference (as opposed to directional) enquiries involve providing advice on a range of sources, or assistance with information strategies, and hence can be handled in a number of ways. To use the testing method to evaluate the whole of the service implies that enquiry work is more straightforward that it actually is. Since what really matters is the customer perspective, the best way to assess the effectiveness of the enquiry service - its timeliness, comprehensiveness, and relevance to need - is to ask the customer.

Reference and enquiry work is an expensive service, since traditionally it employs professionally-qualified staff; being a demand-led service it can at times be inefficient, as it is difficult accurately to match the level of service provision with the extent and intensity of demand. From time to time library managers may wish to look at the cost-effectiveness of different profiles of service provision. In such instances cost-benefit analyses, which evaluate the satisfaction felt with the service in relation to the costs of providing it, possibly using different grades and types of staff, can assist in establishing the most appropriate option.

Current awareness service/SDI service

Definition and scope
Provision of tailored information to customers on new publications received/new articles published/new information on specific topics of interest/relevance.

Performance indicators

Market penetration:	subscribers as proportion of potential subscribers
Effectiveness:	surveys of needs fill rate (user satisfaction)
	percentage of repeat use
Cost-effectiveness:	cost of service per subscriber of different standards
	of production
Costs:	cost per bulletin produced
Productivity:	bulletins produced per relevant member of staff

This is an example of a service which is likely to be one of the key services provided by a commercial or other special library. The best way of assessing the effectiveness of such a service (in terms of its relevance, coverage, timeliness and frequency) is to ask the customers. It may be equally important to ask those who do not use the service the reasons for their non-use. This would apply also to a number of other services listed above, such as information skills training, on-line searching and so on.

7. How to develop performance indicators

Involving staff

The development of performance indicators should not be seen as isolated from the normal processes of management, nor should they be developed by one person, single-handed.

The value of involving staff in planning and decision making, and of encouraging ideas generation at all levels, is now widely recognised. Concepts such as team management, and the gradual change in perception of the manager's role from autocratic decision maker to mentor and coach are reflections of changing perceptions in society generally; they are also acknowledgements of the fact that management decisions are likely to be better, and better accepted, if staff are given an opportunity to contribute their ideas and views. In addition, people tend to feel more allegiance to those decisions to which they have had an input, and they are more likely to own the consequences of any decisions in which they have been involved.

How to get started

As with any other project, one of the most difficult steps in the development of performance indicators is how to get started.

The exact process which the library manager adopts will be influenced to a large extent by the local situation. It is however important to devote as much time and thought to the process to be adopted as to the details of the task itself: sufficient consideration must be given to the 'human' aspects of the project at the outset.

Factors to consider when deciding how to introduce performance measurement include:-

1. Strategic objectives: are up-to-date objectives articulated and understood by all the staff?

2. To what extent have staff been involved in project work before?

3. How will such project work be organised alongside the day to day operations of running the library and maintaining services?

4.   Who will take charge of project development?

5.   How much do staff already know and understand about performance measurement?

6.   What is the attitude of different groups of staff likely to be?

As has been discussed in chapter 4, consideration of question 1 is fundamental to the successful development of performance indicators. If no recent work has been undertaken in this area, then time and effort should be directed towards this at the outset. Even if strategic objectives have been established and agreed, it is still valuable to start any work on performance indicators with some refresher sessions, reminding staff of the strategic aims, in order to set the exercise in context.

The extent to which staff have been involved in project work in the past will determine the approach to be adopted, the amount of ground which will need to be prepared beforehand, and the speed at which the project can be expected to progress. Staff who are used to participating in project groups will find it easier to become involved in such an exercise than those who are unused to operating in this way. It may not be immediately obvious how project group meetings can be organised around the day to day work of the service, particularly in small libraries, so guidance from a senior manager may be required here on when groups should meet and how much time staff should devote to the exercise. For some staff, especially but not exclusively junior staff, the notion that their opinions and ideas are sought by those more senior to themselves can be entirely foreign, particularly if in the past their role has simply been to 'get on with the job'. Such staff will need time and constant encouragement. Thought may also need to be given to providing some skills training, for example in areas such as time management, how to contribute to meetings, and how to take minutes of meetings.

The need for such training should not however be used as a reason for delaying commencement of work on performance indicators. Rather than provide all the training staff may require before initiating the exercise, it is better for training to run alongside the project work itself, so that action and learning go hand in hand.

Question 4 refers to the need to give thought to coordination and control of the project. An exercise of this nature must be given strong, unequivocal support from the most senior library manager; if this work can also be endorsed by the person or committee in the organisation to which the chief librarian reports, then this too is a valuable signal to staff of the importance attached to it.

However interested the senior library manager is in performance measurement it is unlikely that, in any except the smallest of libraries, he or she will have the time to act as project coordinator on a day to day basis. It is therefore recommended that one member of staff be appointed to this role. In large libraries there may be a project officer, sometimes called Research Librarian, or Development Librarian, to whom such a responsibility may naturally fall. Where this is the case, it is still important to make it clear that support and guidance from senior management are always available.

In smaller libraries which do not have the advantage of a dedicated project support post, a project coordinator will need to be appointed from among the existing staff. Although the member of staff selected is likely to be at a fairly senior level in order to have the breadth of experience and expertise needed for such a role, aptitude, enthusiasm and the ability to motivate others are as important as seniority.

The exact role of the project coordinator will depend to a large extent on the answer to questions 2 and 3 above. Staff who are relatively inexperienced at working in teams and groups will need the project coordinator to act primarily as coach and guide, suggesting approaches and providing encouragement. Staff who are more experienced in this style of working may principally require someone to monitor progress, to gather and retain the data collected, and to act as a two-way channel of communication with senior management.

The senior manager must have a clear idea as to the exact nature of the project coordinator's role, and spend time discussing the role with the person concerned before taking the exercise further. Whatever the role of the project coordinator, it is not essential for that person to be any sort of 'expert' on performance measurement at the outset; of course he or she may wish to read up on work which has been undertaken elsewhere, and discuss the initiative with colleagues in other libraries. But the exercise is as much a learning experience for the project coordinator and for the senior managers as it is for the rest of the staff.

While it may be fairly straightforward to ascertain how much the library staff understand about performance measurement, it may be more difficult to judge how they might react to its proposed introduction. The language of performance measurement can often appear hard and threatening, and tends to make staff feel that they personally are being judged. Depending on the morale of the staff and the economic health of the organisation, there may also be concern that the exercise is a smoke screen for job cuts.

Potential staff resistance is no reason for not introducing performance indicators. But being prepared for the types of objections staff may have will assist the library manager to find suitable ways to answer their queries and allay their fears. As with any process of change it is essential for the library manager to communicate constantly, to lead and encourage, to invite staff to voice their concerns and reservations and then to consider those concerns seriously and respond to them honestly.

Use of a consultant

In some libraries, particularly those in large public library authorities, impetus for initiating a performance indicator project has been provided by an external consultant. In some cases the whole exercise has been overseen, led and coordinated by a consultant.

Employing a consultant can be a useful way of getting such a project going. As an outsider to the organisation, the consultant can provide a fresh view of the library operation, and can often suggest approaches to the exercise which might not occur to the staff themselves. However, such an approach should not be seen as a substitute for involving the library staff, or as a way of handing over managerial responsibility to someone else. This attitude, whether conscious or unconscious, will quickly communicate itself to the staff, who will then feel no obligation to become involved or take ownership of the project. If undertaken in this way the project will be doomed from the outset. To be of value performance measurement must be integrated into the normal process of management and supervision, as it must continue long after the consultant has been paid and moved on to another assignment.

Approaching the task

Chapter 6 above identified thirteen key service areas which are likely to form the focus of performance measurement in most libraries. In deciding which service area to tackle first, a useful approach is to start with an area which is reasonably straightforward, in which you feel that progress will be relatively quick, offering reasonably swift results and visible successes. This is partly because it is always easier (and more motivating) to start with the more simple and progress gradually to the more difficult. But it is also a good approach in cases where groups of staff remain sceptical and unconvinced. Demonstrating success is an excellent way of gaining converts. Staff will feel more inclined to persevere with complex areas of service if they have already seen the benefits of efforts made in other areas.

To start with an area which poses fewer difficulties normally means a process-based library service (such as acquisitions, cataloguing or inter-library loans) rather than one of the information service areas, since in the latter the tangibles are more difficult to identify and quantify. A further consideration in choosing where to start is the likely attitude of the staff who operate that service. In any library service, there will be groups of staff who work better as teams than others - because of their experience, their level of commitment, or the dynamics of the group. It is of course sensible to start with a service area in which the service manager is enthusiastic about the initiative, since that enthusiasm will communicate itself to the section staff.

There is another, complementary, way of identifying where to start which has been used in at least one performance indicator project (Abbott (15)). That is to start with a 'problem situation' in which all those involved can agree needs to be addressed, and use this as the springboard for the development of performance indicators. In the example referred to above, the backlog in the cataloguing department provided the necessary focus. Starting with such an issue had the advantage that all the staff in the section were agreed that this was a problem; it was easy to demonstrate that existing data collection routines and management initiatives were not succeeding in eradicating the problem, or keeping it under control, and hence that new methods needed to be found.

Before embarking on detailed work, it is necessary to decide on the nature and composition of the work team. Factors such as the overall number of staff involved in providing the service and their distribution across one or more locations will affect the composition of the team. The maximum manageable size of group will depend on local constraints but should not normally be more than eight. Ideally teams should be composed of staff at different levels.

Once the service area and the work group have been identified, detailed work must begin. As with any new assignment, the work seems less daunting when it is broken down into subtasks. The Performance Indicator Route Map in Figure 3   provides an outline of the suggested stages in any performance measurement exercise. Figure 9 amplifies stages 4 to 9 of the route map and offers a twelve-step approach which a library could adopt in order to tackle the development of performance indicators.

The recommended list of stages in Figure 9 assumes that the staff involved have already been briefed on the reasons for developing performance indicators, the nature of the exercise and their role within it, in broad terms. It is also assumed that they have had an opportunity to discuss any uncertainties concerning the purpose and application of performance indicators, and that the basic terminology of performance measurement has been explained. A combination of staff meetings and written papers will probably be needed to accomplish this initial briefing stage. It is however essential that these preliminaries be addressed before launching into small working groups.

The first step in Figure 9 is to establish objectives for the service. This ensures that no misunderstandings exist as to the focus of the work in hand, and to highlight differences of perspective which there may be between the staff. For example, in using this approach with the staff in the cataloguing service, one might expect statements of the objective of the service to range from ones which are very user-centred, to ones which focus on the professionalism needed to undertake the cataloguing tasks. A user-oriented definition of the cataloguing service might be 'To provide library users with an accurate, straightforward means of identifying items of library stock by author, title, or subject' while a statement of objective from the provider's point of view might be 'To provide a full and accurate description of all items of library stock according to a set of professional standards'. Both of these definitions could be deemed correct but one might be preferable to the other, depending on the type of library in question. In the majority of cases however definitions of objectives which emphasise the customer's perspective, and indicate the contribution of the service to fulfilling the customer's needs, will be preferable to introspective definitions.

The purpose of the second stage is to draw a distinction between the service provided, and the activities which comprise the totality of that service. For example, the activities which are undertaken as part of the cataloguing service might include identification of a cataloguing record on a database, downloading that record, modifying the record to comply with local standards, and adding local location information. These different activities are not the purpose of the cataloguing service, but they are the elements which are (or should be) essential for that purpose to be achieved. This stage helps to ensure clarity of focus among the group members. For example we might ask: does the 'Acquisitions Service' include materials selection, binding and processing, or are these subfunctions of other services (such as collection development and collection maintenance)? It also serves to highlight any steps in the process which may be unnecessary, or inconsistencies of approach which exist between different staff members. It provides a checklist of processes which can be returned to for more detailed consideration when remedial action needs to be taken (stage 12).

In stages 3, 4 and 5 the inputs, outputs and indicators are defined, in line with the conceptual model illustrated in Figure 5. Most groups will be able to determine in broad terms the inputs and outputs of a service, once the principles have been explained. Group members may also wish to consider stage 6 and propose the indicators to be used. Clearly however this is the stage at which the involvement of a more senior manager will be needed to ensure consistency across all services, and to check that all the relevant indicators are being considered. Similarly, advice would need to be taken on data collection methods and reporting mechanisms (stages 7 and 8). Data collection is discussed further in chapter 8 below.

Depending on the data collection method chosen, and the particular local circumstances, stages 9 to 11 might be carried out by the group itself, by the project coordinator, or by someone else entirely. Whichever approach is used it is nevertheless important that the working group be kept regularly informed of progress, and that it receives early reports of any findings arising from the analyses. The experience of the staff will be needed at stage 12 when, in the light of the performance analysis, explanations are needed for the findings and remedial action that needs to be taken.

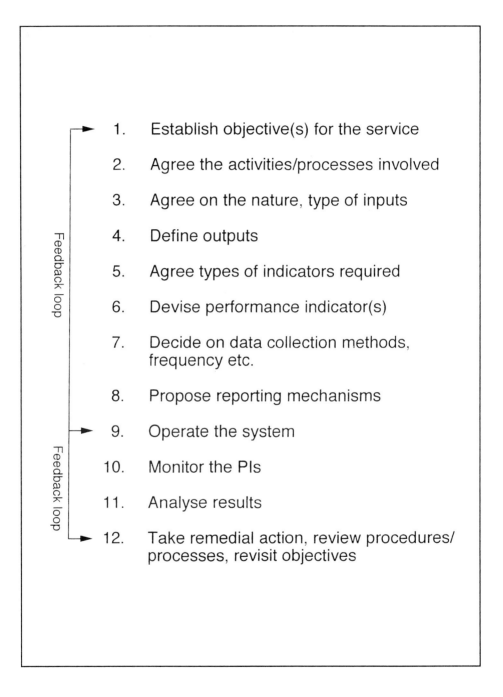

Figure 9 - Stages in the development of performance indicators

Stage 12 is of vital importance. However comprehensive and thorough the performance measurement has been, its value is either made or lost at this stage. The action which should be taken as a result of performance analysis is a matter of management judgement, and will depend on the nature of the findings, the importance attributed to the service within the library operation as a whole, and the cost (or effort) required to implement changes. Clearly any proposed action will require consultation, with the staff operating the service, with staff in other sections who might be indirectly affected by any changes in procedures, and with other service managers.

As the feedback loops in Figure 9 suggest, it may be necessary to repeat performance analyses a number of times before deciding on the appropriate action to take. And the effect of any remedial action taken should be tested by further data gathering exercises. If performance falls a long way short of what is expected or desired, then it may also be necessary to revisit the service objectives, and reconsider the level and nature of the inputs to that service. For as Figure 9 indicates, the process of performance measurement is not a linear but an iterative one, by which performance is refined and constantly improved.

8. Data collection and analysis

Sources of data

Internal systems data

The prevalence of computerised systems in libraries means that much of the data required for performance measurement is now generated and collected automatically as part of normal library housekeeping routines. For example, library circulation systems have the potential to provide quite sophisticated performance information on stock use, such as numbers of loans per item within different categories, the proportion of stock used or not used in a given period, and details of issue transactions by service point or type of transaction. Some systems can provide statistics on active borrowers as distinct from registered but non-active ones. Similarly, computerised inter-library loans, acquisitions and cataloguing systems can provide quantitative data on activity levels and supply times, - data which will be needed for a range of indicators. Electronic information services, both on-line services and CD-ROM, often cumulate usage statistics and cost information automatically. However, such data normally needs to be downloaded to a PC before it can be analysed and used in any meaningful way for performance measurement..

Internally-generated data

A great deal of performance data, although not automatically available, can be obtained by the library by means of simple counts, or observations. Data of this sort will include:

- occupancy counts (eg to ascertain percentage seat occupancy in the library, or use of different service areas in the library)

- observation of queues (eg to ascertain average, maximum and minimum waiting times for services)

- random sample shelf checks (eg to determine the accuracy of reshelving)

- counts of users of services, such as an SDI service

- number of requests for certain types of information eg share prices, bank rates, etc.

In some instances special routines will need to be established to collect the data required. Delay analyses (of inter-library loans, or acquisition services) and studies of the speed and timeliness of delivery are examples. Collecting the required data is more likely to become part of the daily routine of staff if it can be combined with the procedures used in undertaking the job itself, rather than by using a separate form or record sheet. So, for example, an academic library which wishes to carry out a delay analysis of the acquisitions process could adapt its purchase request stationery to enable the information required to be recorded on the form itself. Figure 10 shows a stock recommendation card which has been modified so that performance data can be recorded on the reverse. By this method, the delays at different stages in the acquisitions process can be identified and analysed.

Delay times in a cataloguing process can be recorded by placing a different coloured slip in the books passed through for cataloguing each day or each week; delay analyses of reshelving can use differently labelled trolleys to identify the items returned for shelving each day.

External data
The range of external data, or environmental statistics, which is needed was discussed in chapter 6. It will include data available from elsewhere in the institution, such as population data, as well as that available from sources outside, such as external indices of book and journal prices, and information about other similar libraries' costs and performance.

Information from users
Much of the information required for effectiveness indicators can only be obtained from users themselves. This applies to the whole area of needs fill rate studies, and user satisfaction information. Collecting this type of data is time-consuming and its interpretation is often complex. Methods of obtaining user feedback are discussed later in this chapter.

Data collection

How often data is collected and how often it is analysed for performance measurement depend upon the nature of the service being measured. In analyses for which the data is collected automatically, (such as turnstile counts of library visits, or issue statistics), it is normally possible for the data to be collected on a daily basis, but to analyse the cumulated file only once a year. Some delay analyses (for example of acquisitions or inter-library loans processes) may lend themselves better to sampling, for example by a study of all transactions for a period of one month, or by a selective study carried out on specific days, repeated on a quarterly or half yearly basis. In areas where special routines need to be instigated to capture the data required, a balance needs to be struck between comprehensiveness and accuracy: continuous data collection will yield more comprehensive data, but accuracy may be reduced, as staff tire of the exercise. More accurate recording of data may be obtained by sampling but this introduces the risk of sampling error, as described later in this chapter.

Stock recommendation card

PLEASE COMPLETE IN BLOCK CAPITALS

New title ☐   New edition ☐   Additional copy/copies ☐

Author

Title

Publisher

ISBN Hbk   Pbk

Date   Edition   Price

Copies required/
Loan category

Course/
Module no.

Name

Library barcode no.

Department/
Mailing
address

Notify + hold ☐   Notify only ☐

Item now added to stock at

....

Loan copy available for you to collect from the
Service Counter. Collect before

....

Front ↑

Reverse ↓

FOR LIBRARY USE ONLY		
RECEIVED BY SUBJECT SPECIALISTS	RECEIVED IN ACQUISITIONS	BIB CHECKED
SUPPLIER ADDED	STATUS CHECKED	DOWNLOADED
ORDERED	RECEIPTED	SENT TO BINDING
SHELVED IN CATALOGUING	SENT TO PROCESSING	COMPLETED

Figure 10 - Stock recommendation card

Any method of performance measurement which involves asking users for their views is time-consuming to administer and analyse, and so the frequency of in-house surveys will depend upon the resources available to the library. In addition, too frequent surveying can lead to 'questionnaire fatigue' on the part of those being surveyed. For this reason it is important to maximise the benefit derived from user surveys by only asking for that information which it is not possible to acquire any other way. Methods of obtaining feedback from users are discussed later in this chapter.

Information on staff costs
In order to measure staff costs associated with specific services the library manager needs to know how much time is devoted to providing each service. In libraries where staff are timetabled for certain sections or services, the timetables can form the basis for assessing the amount of staff time spent on different activities. Where this is not the case, there are three alternative methods:

- random observation of staff

- asking staff and their supervisors to estimate the proportion of time spent on different services

- use of daily time logging sheets, to be completed by each individual concerned, either on a continuous or a periodic basis. The headings used and the number of services or functions across which staff are asked to log their time will depend on the type of library, the level of detail required for performance measurement, and the level of staff involved.

Whatever method is used to obtain information on staff time, decisions need to be made on how to treat the costs of training time and other non-operational time such as meetings; the apportionment of management overheads; whether to use actual salary points or mid-points of a grade, and what level of employer on-costs need to be added to the gross salary. Whichever method is chosen it is important that it should be implemented consistently. Sometimes organisations have their own management accounting conventions for service costings, which the library would be wise to follow. Alternatively, brief, useful guidance can be found in King Research Ltd (10).

Feedback from users
The three main methods of obtaining user feedback are user satisfaction questionnaires, interviews and group discussions. Interviews are most appropriate in cases where qualitative information is required, for example on satisfaction levels with a specific service. The interviews should be brief, ideally no more than four or five questions. It is important that in every case the question is asked in the same way, to reduce the possibility of distortion in the results. There are a variety of interview types, from the structured, through the semi-structured, to the in-depth interview. Interviews can be conducted by telephone, or in person. Which type and method to use will depend on the nature of the subject matter and the questions being asked. (For further guidance on interview techniques, see Slater (16)).

Group discussions can be used to obtain subjective evaluation of services, but they are not often used as means of obtaining performance indicator information. The technique is more appropriate as a means of obtaining in-depth qualitative information from a small number of targeted users and hence can provide valuable information in support of effectiveness indicators, for example by providing reasons for the evaluations given in questionnaires (Pocklington and Finch, (17)).

Questionnaires are the most commonly used tool for eliciting feedback from customers. The frequency with which they are used suggests a misguided belief in the minds of librarians that questionnaires are simple to design, quick to administer and easy to interpret. In reality, this is often far from the case. While there is insufficient space in this guide to examine questionnaire design in any detail, the following points should help librarians to decide whether use of a questionnaire is appropriate or not. King Research Ltd (10) offers four basic rules of questionnaire design:

- ask only questions which are capable of being answered

- ask the minimum of information required (ie ask what is essential to know, not what would be nice to know)

- ask only those questions which can be realistically (and truthfully) answered

- ask only those questions which customers will be prepared to answer.

Given the high cost of administering questionnaires, one more rule should be added to this list:

- only ask for information which is unobtainable by any other means.

The method of recording and interpreting the data received should be considered at the questionnaire design stage. For large numbers of responses the most manageable way to deal with the data is to use a computer package designed for the analysis of statistical data, such as SAS, for use on a mainframe computer, a PC-based package such as Minitab, or SPSS which exists in both mainframe and PC versions. If such a package is to be used, the questions should be precoded as described in the software manuals to enable the data to be input quickly and easily in the required format.

A large number of texts are available giving advice on survey methods and questionnaire design. See for example Slater (16) and Line (19).

Sampling
Given the large amounts of data with which libraries deal, it is often the case that performance studies need to be undertaken on the basis of samples, rather than analysis of the entire population. This applies whether the 'population' in question consists of items of stock, issues, on-line searches conducted, or the human 'population' of users.

Care needs to be taken when using a sample to ensure that the data obtained is relatively free from bias and sufficiently precise to be of use: in other words you must have confidence that the results of the sample can be used to make inferences about the population as a whole. The aspects of sampling which should be considered are: the sample frame; the sampling method; and sample size.

Sampling frame
The sampling frame is, quite simply, a list of the whole population from which the survey sample will be selected, eg the file of registered users in a comprehensive user survey, or the list of days when a delivery survey is being undertaken.

Sampling methods
The simplest method is random sampling, which consists of using random numbers to identify and select sampling units from the sample frame. This would be an appropriate technique to use in an analysis of delivery times (for example of inter-library loan requests, or transactions at an issues or enquiry desk).

A systematic random sample can be used when the units in the sampling frame themselves occur in a truly random, non-purposive way, such as for example the enquiries received by an enquiry service. Systematic random sampling means that a random number is used to determine the sampling interval; so every, say, fifth customer could be surveyed.

In some situations a combination of sampling techniques could be appropriate. For a survey of enquiries, random numbers could be used to select the days on which the survey will be conducted, and within each day systematic sampling could be used to choose the customers to be interviewed.

Sample size
The size of a sample depends upon a number of factors, such as the size of the population, the nature of the enquiry and of the data (whether it is qualitative or quantitative), and the accuracy of results required. Generally speaking the larger the sample, the more reliable are the results. For more information on sampling, see Simpson (20). Formulae for calculating sample sizes are given in Slater (16) and in Carpenter and Vasu (21).

How to organise and manage your data

One of the more difficult aspects of performance evaluation is how to organise the quantities of data collected. As with any project, performance measurement can generate large amounts of paper, and it is easy to become overwhelmed, particularly if the task of collating, manipulating and analysing this data falls primarily to one person. Try to ensure that data is gathered in an order and a format which facilitates data entry, then this will speed up the task considerably.

There is no easy solution to the problems of data organisation, but the following tips can be given:-

- Transfer data to computer-based spreadsheets

- Enlist the assistance of other staff

- Provide networked access

- Disseminate data summaries and progress reports via newsletters and bulletins.

Analysing performance data

Use of statistical methods enables the librarian undertaking performance measurement to move from the analysis stage of the process (Stage 11 on Figure 9), to the final, and arguably most important, stage - remedial action. Some understanding of the use and value of statistical methods is essential for anyone undertaking performance measurement. The point to remember is that statistical techniques help the researcher to make sense of data, to compare different sets of findings and to determine the significance of results. It is however important for statistical tests to be applied appropriately. The indiscriminate application of statistical techniques is as dangerous as not using them at all, and both can both lead to spurious conclusions.

There are a large number of statistical techniques which are potentially relevant to anyone carrying out performance measurement studies. A number of good books on statistics have been written specifically for librarians (20, 21, 22); issues concerning the analysis of quantitative and qualitative data are discussed in Slater (16), while Line (19) provides some very useful guidance on statistical techniques in relation to surveys, as well as comprehensive lists of further reading. King Research Ltd (10) also includes a short section on statistical methods.

Presenting your findings

Presenting the findings of performance analyses in ways which are interesting and readily comprehensible is as important as collecting the data itself; for data which does not appear useful or applicable will not be used. So, raw data needs to be collated, summarised and organised, and presented in a way which attracts the attention of the reader. This often means presenting it in a graphical form. Let us take the example of an analysis of acquisitions supply times for monographs. The type of data elements which would be required for such an analysis include the date the item is ordered, the date it is received and the supplier's name. From this data the number of working days taken to supply each item can be calculated.

Even on a small data file, it is impossible to draw any conclusions from such data when it is presented as a simple list. So the first step might be to group the data by supplier and then reorganise it in ascending order of supply times in order to show the longest and shortest supply times; then to calculate the mean average supply time. But grouping the data in this way makes it only marginally easier to understand; as a bar chart (Figure 11) it is much more easily comprehensible.

In this example grouping data by supplier and presenting it as cumulative bar charts allows proportions, (the proportion of items from different suppliers which arrived within a given number of days), to be compared, and hence any actual or potential problem areas to be identified quickly. Other survey results may lend themselves to presentation in the form of pie charts, histograms and scatter diagrams. (Note that the tables of raw data should also be available, since some graphical displays obscure detail which can be needed in order to pursue the analyses further.) Many spreadsheet packages now have an automatic graphics facility which greatly simplifies the production of charts of various sorts. (For more guidance on the presentation of data, see Line (19), and Simpson (22)).

However neither tables nor charts are likely to suffice on their own. In almost all cases statistical data, in whatever form it is presented, should be supplemented by text. This should explain the methodology of the exercise, and the period of time covered; it should highlight any aspects of performance to which the results point, and suggest action or further analysis which needs to be undertaken.

Once performance measurement is established and has become part of the regular cycle of management activity in the library, it is best for performance data to be integrated into regular management reports (Abbott, (15)). Senior management will require summary information on performance, and only need recourse to detail in cases where they are concerned over certain aspects. For middle managers, performance information can help them to prioritise different tasks, and to allocate staff resources in the most appropriate way - ie it helps them to take a range of short-term management decisions which will optimise the performance of the service.

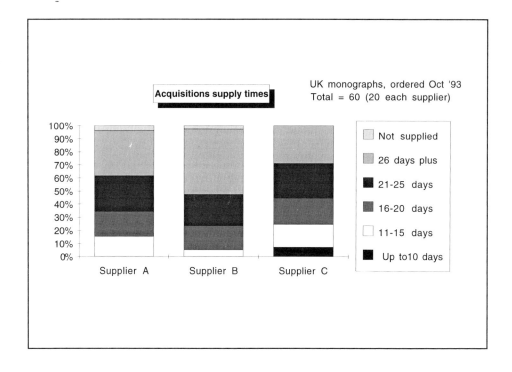

Figure 11 - Acquisitions supply times

9. Conclusion

This guide has sought to provide a practical introduction to performance measurement in library and information services for those with little or no previous experience of the subject. Performance measurement has already been extensively debated and the complexity of that discussion has been partly to blame for the confusion felt by many who are seeking to come to grips with the topic. This guide has attempted to strip away some of that complexity and to provide readers with a step-by-step approach which can be tailored to the circumstances prevailing in their particular library environments.

The fact that the original reason for introducing performance indicators has in many cases been a defensive one should not be allowed to obscure the genuine benefit which the systematic use of performance indicators can bring. The most persuasive argument in favour of performance measurement is simply that it is part of good management practice. Performance indicators should be seen, not as something special, but essential as tools in the good manager's toolkit.

Much of the writing on performance measurement has concentrated on the detailed or the peripheral - the types of indicators libraries can adopt, the exact meaning of different indicators, and the external threats to which performance indicators are a response - that the profession has tended to lose sight of the ultimate purpose of the exercise - namely, the systematic improvement of library services. For this improvement to take place the services provided must be subject to continual critical evaluation, and the library manager must constantly look for ways of improving the efficiency, effectiveness and value for money offered by the library service. The integrated use of performance indicators will assist the library manager in this process of evaluation and improvement.

If handled sensitively, the introduction of performance measurement can be a positive development for any library, helping to sharpen up objectives, encouraging staff commitment, and facilitating the development of new skills. Performance indicators help the correct decisions to be made, but are no substitute for professional judgement.

Fashions in management practice have changed considerably since performance measurement was first discussed in libraries. Some librarians might be tempted to think that performance measurement is now redundant. This guide has sought to demonstrate that, on the contrary, a sound system of performance measurement complements many more recent management approaches; the introduction of initiatives such as Quality management and Customer charters is likely to be smoother and the outcome more successful if they are underpinned by information derived from performance indicators.

Libraries are, above all, services for people. Although any system of performance measurement must involve the use of numbers, these are only of value if they help the library manager to achieve quality of service for users.

References

1   Goodall, D.L. Performance measurement: a historical perspective. *Journal of Librarianship,* 1988, 20 (2) pp128-144.

2   Blagden, J. and J. Harrington. *How good is your library? A review of approaches to the evaluation of library and information services.* London: Aslib, 1990.

3   Winkworth, I. *Performance measurement and performance indicators. In* Collection management in academic libraries, edited by C. Jenkins and M. Morley. Aldershot: Gower, 1991. pp57-93.

4   Zweizig, D.L. So go figure: measuring library effectiveness. *Public Libraries,* 1987, 26 (1) pp 21-24.

5   Orr, R.H. Measuring the goodness of library services: a general framework for considering quantitative measures. *Journal of Documentation,* 1993, 29 pp 315-332.

6   Committee of Vice-Chancellors and Principals. *University management statistics and performance indicators, UK universities.* London: CVCP, 1987.

7   Winkworth, I.R. Performance indicators for polytechnic libraries. *Library Review,* 1990, 39 (5) pp23 - 41.

8   *Performance indicators for university libraries: a practical guide.* London: Standing Conference on National and University Libraries, 1992.

9   Sumsion, J. *Practical performance indicators - 1992. Documenting the Citizens' Charter consultation for U.K. public libraries with examples of PIs and surveys in use.* Loughborough: Library and Information Statistics Unit, 1993.

10   King Research Ltd. *Keys to success: performance indicators for public libraries.* (Library Information series no. 18). London: Office of Arts and Libraries, 1990.

11   Lancaster, F.W. *If you want to evaluate your library...* London: Library Association, 1988.

12   Meadows, J. *Why do librarians not use performance measures? In* Performance measures of public services: papers presented at a seminar in Stamford, Lincolnshire in March 1988, edited by Royston Brown and Hilary Spiers. Stamford: Capital Planning Information, 1988.

13   Brophy, P. Performance measurement in academic libraries: a polytechnic perspective. *British Journal of Academic Librarianship,* 1989, 4 (2) pp99-110.

14   Ford, G. Approaches to performance measurement: some observations on principles and practice. *British Journal of Academic Librarianship,* 1989, 4 (2) pp74 - 87.

15   Abbott, C. What does good look like? The adoption of performance indicators at Aston University Library and Information Services. *British Journal of Academic Librarianship,* 1990, 5 (2), pp79 - 94.

16   Slater, M (ed). *Research methods in library and information studies.* London: The Library Association, 1990.

17   Pocklington, K. and H. Finch. *Research collections under constraint: the effect on researchers. Academics' perceptions of the impact on the research process of constraints to library budgets: a qualitative study.* (British Library Research paper 36). London: British Library Research and Development Department, 1987.

18   Mann, P.H. *Methods of social investigation.* Oxford: Blackwell, 1985.

19   Line, M. B. *Library surveys: an introduction to the use, planning, procedure and presentation of surveys. 2nd ed.,* revised by Sue Stone. London: Bingley, 1982.

20   Simpson, I.S. *Basic statistics for librarians, 3rd ed.* London: Library Association Publishing, 1988.

21   Carpenter, R.L. and E.S. Vasu. *Statistical methods for librarians.* Chicago: American Library Association, 1978.

22   Simpson, I.S. *How to interpret statistical data: a guide for librarians and information scientists.* London: Library Association Publishing, 1990.